D1333215

3 0116 02028390 7

GYMNASTICS
VAULTING
Tips, Rules and Legendary Stars

by Tracy Nelson Maurer

Consultant:
Julie Belemore
WA Senior Club Coach
Secretary Essex Gymnastics Association
BSGA Regional Judging Convenor

raintree
a Capstone company — publishers for children

Raintree is an imprint of Capstone Global Library Limited, a company incorporated in England and Wales having its registered office at 264 Banbury Road, Oxford, OX2 7DY – Registered company number: 6695582

www.raintree.co.uk
myorders@raintree.co.uk

Text © Capstone Global Library Limited 2017
The moral rights of the proprietor have been asserted.

All rights reserved. No part of this publication may be reproduced in any form or by any means (including photocopying or storing it in any medium by electronic means and whether or not transiently or incidentally to some other use of this publication) without the written permission of the copyright owner, except in accordance with the provisions of the Copyright, Designs and Patents Act 1988 or under the terms of a licence issued by the Copyright Licensing Agency, Saffron House, 6–10 Kirby Street, London EC1N 8TS (www.cla.co.uk). Applications for the copyright owner's written permission should be addressed to the publisher.

Edited by Gena Chester
Designed by Bobbie Nuytten
Picture research by Kelly Garvin
Production by Tori Abraham
Printed in China.

ISBN 978 1 4747 2634 4
20 19 18 17 16
10 9 8 7 6 5 4 3 2 1

British Library Cataloguing in Publication Data
A full catalogue record for this book is available from the British Library.

Acknowledgements
We would like to thank the following for permission to reproduce photographs: Capstone Press: Karon Dubke, 7, 8, 10, 11, 14, 15, 16, 17, Martin Bustamante, 22, 23; Getty Images/Jean-Loup Gautreau/AFP, 28; iStockphoto: Brain McEntire, cover, 6, 18; Kelly Garvin, 20; Newscom: Ai Wire Photo Service, 26, David C. Turnley/KRT, 27, David Eulitt/KRT, 19, Jeff Siner/MCT, 25, Mike Blake/Reuters, 29; Shutterstock: Aspen Photo, 1, Brendan Howard, 12, ID1974, 13, Lilyana Vynogradova, 5, 21, Paolo Bona, 9

Artistic Elements: Shutterstock: alexdndz, Hakki Arslan, kayannl

Every effort has been made to contact copyright holders of material reproduced in this book. Any omissions will be rectified in subsequent printings if notice is given to the publisher.

All the internet addresses (URLs) given in this book were valid at the time of going to press. However, due to the dynamic nature of the internet, some addresses may have changed, or sites may have changed or ceased to exist since publication. While the author and publisher regret any inconvenience this may cause readers, no responsibility for any such changes can be accepted by either the author or the publisher.

Contents

Leapfrog
with a horse

Imagine a game of extreme leapfrog, and you're close to the thrill of the vault in gymnastics. To vault means to jump over something. Gymnasts use a **springboard** to launch their jump toward an **apparatus** called a horse or vaulting table. **Blocking** helps these gymnasts fly high up into the air – up to 2.4 metres (8 feet) – for spectacular tricks.

Vaulting is an artistic gymnastics event. Some artistic gymnastic events are for only men and some are for only women. For example, only women compete in balance beam and uneven bars. Men compete in still rings, pommel horse, high bar, and parallel bars. But both genders compete in vault and floor exercise events.

Gymnasts perform the vault with one or more moves in a fast series while in the air. Don't blink! The entire vault is over in seconds. But it can take months to learn a new move and even longer to polish the entire vault from start to finish. The amazing vaults at the Olympics begin with countless hours of practice and exercises.

Fast fact:

Ancient Romans used a wooden horse to teach mounts and dismounts. Gymnastics borrowed this idea for the early vault apparatus, but today's vaulting table replaced this apparatus in 2001.

springboard strong, flexible board that is used for jumping very high
apparatus equipment used in gymnastics, such as the vaulting table
block movement where the gymnast pushes off the vaulting table to gain distance and height for his or her move

Chapter 1

Ready, set, vault!

Vault practice should only be done at a gym or club with adult supervision. There, experienced coaches and the best equipment create a safe environment. In the United Kingdom, many clubs are affiliated with British Gymnastics. Visit British Gymnastics' official website to find clubs near you.

Vaulting work means sweaty practices at the gymnastics gym. A coach or trainer needs to stand nearby every time you practise a vault. They are ready to protect a gymnast from a fall. Before you start practising skills on the block, you need to be prepared. And that includes showing up ready to work.

Gymnastics garb

For training and competition, boys and girls must wear close-fitting clothing that won't catch on the apparatus. Girls wear one-piece stretchy suits called **leotards** for practise and competition.

For practice, girls may choose to wear close-fitting shorts with their leotards. They also pull their hair back in a ponytail or a high bun. Boys can wear shorts and T-shirts for practises. They also have the choice to dress as they would for competition. Boys compete in a **singlet** with short over the top.

leotard snug, one-piece garment worn by gymnasts and dancers
singlet one-piece, sleeveless garment worn mostly by males for gymnastics, wrestling and exercise

Table talk

A vaulting table measures approximately 120 centimetres (3.9 feet) long by 95 centimetres (3.1 feet) wide for both men and women. The sloped front makes blocking safer for gymnasts. A padded surface absorbs shock to help avoid shoulder and wrist injuries. Women vault the table at approximately 125 centimetres high (4.1 feet). Men use it at 135 centimetres high (4.4 feet).

Preflight

Gymnasts practise running hard down the padded runway to gain **momentum.** They bring their knees up high and keep their elbows close to the body.

Gymnasts also work on their step from the springboard to the table. They jump hard with both feet onto the springboard's surface to launch themselves into the air. Some gymnasts perform a **round off** instead of a **hurdle** on to the board. Once they've landed the round off, they propel from the springboard toward the table using a back handspring.

The part of the vault from the springboard up until the gymnast's hands reach the apparatus is called the **preflight**. Any preflight trick, such as the back handspring, should place the gymnast in the correct position for the block. Hands come to the table flat and shoulder-width apart. The rest of the body aligns with the shoulders. Elbows stay straight. Ankles stay together in the preflight while the hands are in contact with the table.

Fast fact:
Men have competed in the vault at the Olympics since 1896. Women began competing individually in the event in 1952.

momentum force or speed created by movement
round off skill similar to a cartwheel but with both feet landing at the same time
hurdle to run and jump onto the springboard
preflight upward lift from the springboard toward the vault table

Postflight

From the block, the **postflight** shows off the gymnast's skills high in the air. Greater height from the block allows more time for tricks with complex twists and flips.

postflight upward lift from the block at the vault table

Landing

The vault ends with the landing. To stick the landing, feet should sink into the mat no more than shoulder-width apart. Bent knees absorb the impact. Arms straight out with palms down help add balance and prevent wobbling. Any additional steps lose points from judges. The gymnast immediately strikes a final pose with legs straight, back arched, chin up, and arms high.

Train for speed and power

Vaulting requires speed and power. A typical workout includes a warm up, apparatus practice, and conditioning. Some conditioning workouts are:

- chin-ups, pull-ups, and push-ups to increase arm strength
- sit-ups and planks that work the core muscles for tight flips and controlled landings
- plyometric jumps, such as small jumps on a mini-trampoline that build power and explosiveness for hurdles

Chapter 2

Block
talk

Gymnasts strive for good form. They control every body movement so that their performances appear easy and graceful. They work on building powerful blocks and explosive launches from the table.

Fast fact:
Gymnasts nicknamed the vaulting table "the tongue" for its curvy shape.

Judges watch the height or **amplitude** gymnasts rise from the table. The distance gymnasts propel away from the table matters in competitions. If the judges think a gymnast's amplitude and distance aren't great enough, they will deduct points. How do gymnasts improve amplitude and distance? Practise, practise, practise!

amplitude height a gymnast reaches from a block off the vault

An experienced vault coach moves each gymnast step by step from basic skills toward difficult tricks. Skipping to a harder trick before you're ready could stunt your confidence or worse, cause an injury.

Fall right

Every gymnast falls countless times when learning new skills. The trick is to fall safely. Practise safety rolls to absorb the impact of a fall. Roll in a tuck position in the direction you're already moving. Don't try to stop your momentum. Make sure your fingers don't catch and bend the wrong way. Cross your arms closely across your chest or put them over your head. Keep your chin down.

The courage vault

Coaches often start with this skill to help gymnasts fight their fears of the vault. Jump hard onto the springboard and land feet first on the table in a tuck position. With knees up to your chest, jump off the table onto the mat. The goal is to practise good form throughout each part of the vault.

Learning new moves takes time. Think of the gymnast's body as making shapes like letters. Mastering these shapes sets the foundation for adding more difficult moves later.

Layout

The gymnast stretches the body into a long line. His or her back stays straight or slightly arched. Think of a capital I.

Pike

The gymnast bends at the hips, stretching the legs straight out in front like a capital L.

Tuck

The gymnast tucks both legs up to the chest as if making a letter O.

The various skills and tricks in vaulting build from these basic letter positions. Just as joined-up handwriting uses lines to connect letters, gymnasts add movements to link one position to another. Spins, twists, and flips add flair. Every gymnast gives his or her vault a touch of personal style.

Chapter 3

Competition

It's important to choose a gymnastics club that fits your goals. British Gymnastics offers the Gymnastics for All program for athletes who do not wish to compete. The program focuses on rewarding gymnastics experiences with less emphasis on training and competition.

Gymnasts with dreams of the Olympics may compete in Elite Compulsory Grades or National Voluntary Levels. These programs have numerous levels based on age and skill. A gymnast must master certain requirements before he or she can move up levels. Once a gymnast is in level 1, he or she may perform in national and international competitions. Then the gymnast might be selected to join the Olympic team.

Fast fact:
Gymnasts must turn 16 in the
calendar year to compete
in the Olympics as a gymnast.

ATHENS 2004

*the 2004 United States Olympic team
after winning the team silver medal*

Gymnasts in levels 5–2 must master **compulsory** moves. Each gymnast performs the same skills exactly the same way. Elite Compulsory Grade level 4 requires gymnasts to perform a straig' front salto from the springboard. Levels 2 and 1 can perform ski' from the various vault styles in an official rule book called the C of Points.

For **elite** competitions, judges look at the difficulty of the vault (D score). Each skill has a difficulty value in the Code of Points. The sum of skill values is equal to the start value or D score. The judges watch the gymnast's form, amplitude, distance and landing to evaluate execution (E score). Execution errors such as knees or ankles apart or extra steps on a landing are subtracted from 10. The remaining total is added with the D score to create a final score.

compulsory required element or routine

elite describes gymnasts who are among the best in the club

Competition wear

Team members compete in matching uniforms. The Code of Points requires matching team tracksuits as well. They wear these during opening ceremonies, at the podium to receive medals, and at closing ceremonies.

Women have specific clothing regulations for competitions. All girls must wear leotards that cover the stomach and back. Leotards should also cover undergarments.

Gymnasts risk losing points for wearing these items:

- T-shirt
- boxer shorts
- headband, cape, or scarf
- jewellery
- straps less than 2 centimetres (¾ inch) wide

Elite gymnasts often choose the skills with the highest difficulty points to increase their scores. The higher start value gives them a bit more room for losing execution points. Coaches guide their choice of skills so that gymnasts have the best chance of attaining the highest possible score.

The Olympics isn't the only event that awards medals. Top scorers at major competitions also earn medals. In these competitions, both male and female gymnasts perform just one vault run, unless it's the individual or team finals. Then gymnasts show two vaults in a row. The average of the two runs determines the gymnast's final score.

Fast fact:
A gymnast must land feet first to be scored for a vault.

medal winners at the 2013 European Championships

Advanced moves

Advanced gymnasts choose performance elements from the vault styles listed as categories in the Code of Points. The most common styles for both men and women include the Yamashita, Tsukahara and Yurchenko.

The Yamashita vault

Haruhiro Yamashita of Japan, a 1964 Olympic men's gold medalist, invented this vault. Gymnasts start with a straight hurdle from the springboard with a front handspring to the table. They pull up to a handstand when their hands reach the table for the block. Most Yamashita vaults feature a post-flight pike off the table. Like the other categories, this move has many variations.

The Tsukahara vault (Tsuk)

This category is named for Mitsuo Tsukahara, a Japanese men's gymnast who competed in three Olympics. Mitsuo won a total of five gold medals from 1968 to 1976. His original vault in 1979 featured a quarter-twist handspring followed by a **salto** backwards in a tuck. Today most gymnasts do a half-twist pre-flight. Gymnasts need a strong jump off the springboard with a tall, tight layout. Gymnasts lift their arms forward and up to the ceiling as they lift and twist onto the table.

The Yurchenko vault

Russian gymnast Natalia Yurchenko first performed this move in 1982. While completing this move, gymnasts have no view of the vault. This is called a blind-entry vault. Gymnasts first sprint down the runway and plant their hands onto a mat set ahead of the springboard. They flip their body into a round off and land both feet onto the springboard. Next they complete a back handspring onto the vault. From the block on the table, gymnasts can perform twists or saltos before sticking the landing. Today almost every Olympic gymnast performs some variation of this blind-entry vault during his or her career.

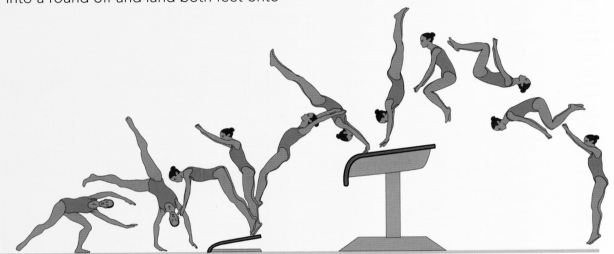

Names in the Code Of Points

The Fédération Internationale de Gymnastique (FIG) creates the Code of Points. Athletes' names are added into the Code of Points when they invent new skills. The skill must be demonstrated at either the Olympics or the Artistic Gymnastics World Championships. If FIG approves it, the group gives the skill the inventor's name in the next Code of Points. An updated rule book comes out every four years.

salto somersault

Competing costs

Competing takes commitment from you and your family. An elite gymnast often trains for 30 hours a week in the gym.

Coaches and parents expect gymnasts to manage their time well, but they know it's hard to balance gymnastics, school and a social life. If you ever feel overwhelmed, find an adult you can talk to about the pressures and expectations. Stay in contact with at least one person who is not involved in the sport to make sure you have friendships and interests beyond the gym.

Competitive gymnasts are also responsible for making good decisions about their health. They eat balanced meals with plenty of protein to build hard-working muscles. Eggs, spinach, cottage cheese and low-fat meats are a few good choices. It's important to avoid skipping meals or following strange diets. This type of behavior is dangerous and can lead to an eating disorder. If you start to worry about your weight, talk to your doctor.

Fast fact:
Famous gymnasts such as Nadia Comaneci, Kathy Johnson and Cathy Rigby have all struggled with eating disorders.

Prep your parents

Family and friends love to cheer you on at competitions, but even they have to follow the rules. Every competition has its own rules. Some common ones are:

- no flash photography
- no food or drinks in the main gym area
- stay out of the competition area and off the equipment unless you are a competitor or a coach
- be respectful and professional observers
- never question a judge

Chapter 4

Legends
of the vault

Gymnastics legends from all over the world have made the sport what it is today. These elite men and women inspire young gymnasts to pursue their own dreams on the vaulting table.

Mary Lou Retton

At the 1984 Los Angeles Olympics, Mary Lou Retton won a silver medal in the team competition and the vault. She also took bronze in the floor exercise and uneven bars. But she became an American gymnastics legend in the all-around competition.

Despite having earned a 10 on the all-around floor exercise, the best score possible at the time, she was still trailing Romanian gymnast Ecaterina Szabo. She needed another perfect 10 on the vault to win. In seconds, Mary Lou wowed the world! She stuck the landing and became the first American woman ever to win a gold medal in gymnastics.

Fast fact:
Mary Lou Retton started gymnastics when she was five years old.

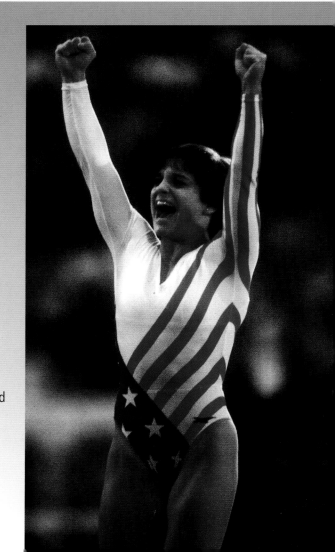

Kerri Strug

Kerri Strug was the youngest athlete to compete in the 1992 Barcelona Olympics. She won a team bronze medal there, but Kerri struggled with injuries and multiple coaches after those Games. She was determined to do well in the 1996 Olympics. She was especially confident on the vault.

By the last day of the Olympic gymnastics team competition in 1996, the Russians were in position to win the gold medal. On the first run, Kerri fell and hurt her ankle badly.

Kerri took her second run. She stuck the landing and saluted the judges on one foot before collapsing in pain. Kerri helped earn the American team a gold medal and became a worldwide star for her courage and team spirit.

Vitaly Scherbo

Vitaly Scherbo grew up in Minsk, Belarus. He loved gymnastics and trained hard for every event. He took the all-around silver at the 1991 World Championships, but he wanted to do better. He came back for the 1992 Olympics in Spain. There Vitaly won six out of a possible eight gold medals in men's gymnastics, including the vault.

By the time he retired after the 1996 Olympics, Vitaly had won four more Olympic bronze medals. He also had earned 23 World Championship medals, including 12 gold medals. No one has earned more World Championship gold medals yet.

Fast fact:
Vitaly Scherbo's full twist onto the vault is listed with his name among the more difficult skills in the Code of Points.

Yang Hak-seon

Yang Hak-seon's nickname is "the God of Vault". At the 2012 Olympic Games, he certainly earned the title.

In 2011 Hak-seon showcased a new vault he invented. The vault, FIG-named "the Yang", is a handspring into a triple twist. When he performed the vault at the 2012 Olympics, it had the highest D-score possible, a 7.4. The vault helped earn him the gold medal in the event.

Hak-seon had hoped to defend his vault title at the 2016 Olympic Games in Rio. He had even developed a new vault, named by fans as the Yang 2. Unfortunately, an Achilles injury in January prevented him from competing in the 2016 Games.

In addition to his Olympic appearance, Hak-seon won two World Championships in the vault event. He was also the first South Korean gymnast to win an Olympic gold medal.

Completing a vault routine takes a lot of hard work, dedication and practice. Gymnastics legends have done all of this to achieve greatness and will inspire you to follow your own dreams. The vault event is a rewarding challenge for all gymnasts.

Glossary

amplitude height a gymnast reaches from a block off the vault

apparatus equipment used in gymnastics, such as the vault table

block movement where the gymnast pushes off the vault table to gain distance and height for his or her move

compulsory required element or routine

elite describes gymnasts who are among the best in the club

hurdle to run and jump onto the springboard

leotard snug, one-piece garment worn by gymnasts and dancers

momentum force or speed created by movement

postflight upward lift from the block at the vault table

preflight upward lift from the springboard toward the vault table

round off skill similar to a cartwheel but with both feet landing at the same time

salto somersault

singlet one-piece, sleeveless garment worn mostly by males for gymnastics, wrestling and exercise

springboard strong, flexible board that is used for jumping very high

Read more

Gymnastics (Mad about), J. Heneghan (Wayland, 2016)

The Gymnastics Book: The Young Performer's Guide to Gymnastics, Elfi Schlegel and Claire Ross Dunn (Firefly, 2012)

The Science Behind Gymnastics (Science of the Summer Olympics), L.E. Carmichael (Raintree, 2016)

Websites

www.british-gymnastics.org
Find a club near where you live and look up lots of information about your favourite British gymnasts

www.fig-gymnastics.com
Find all of the official rules of gymnastics at the website of the Fédération Internationale de Gymnastique (FIG).

www.ukgymnastics.org
Find out all the latest news about gymnastics in the United Kingdom.

INDEX